I Said What I Said

Keetha Johnson

BookLeaf Publishing

I Said What I Said © 2023

Keetha Johnson

Presentation by *BookLeaf Publishing*

Web: www.bookleafpub.com

E-mail: info@bookleafpub.com

ISBN: 978-93-5721-329-5

First edition 2023

I would like to dedicate this collection to anyone and everyone who ever made an impact on my life, positive or negative. Thanks for the inspiration.

ACKNOWLEDGEMENT

I would like to thank the amazing team at Bookleaf Publishing for giving artists a chance to share their masterpieces with the world, especially the ones who might not have been able to otherwise. I would also like to thank my wonderful supporters. I'd be nothing without you.

PREFACE

Round 2: With *spice* this time!

Heart of Gold

My most dedicated fan
My biggest devotee
I can't thank you enough
For supporting me

Always there to pick me up
When I fall flat on my face
Always being proud of me
No matter what I place

First or last
You pay no mind
You're always quick
To help me find

The silver lining in it all
To pull me out of my despair
You've seen me at my very worst
But never seem to care

To you it makes no difference
You love me all the same
Despite my endless flaws
Or how I drive you insane

I would not have made it

To where I am today
Without your gentle hand
To help me on my way

Without your patience and your humour
Your quick wit and that smile
Your understanding and compassion
Your want to walk a mile

Wearing someone else's shoes
So you can better understand
Why some people are a product
Of a life not lived as planned

With a heart made of pure gold
And a want to keep on growing
Even on your worst days
Your halo's always glowing

I don't know what it was I did
For me to get so lucky
To have such an amazing person
Decide he wants to love me.

Hush

Do you even know
What you're talking about
Or does the thought cross your mind
And you just let it out

Do you even consider
The effect of your words
Who you might offend
Or who you might hurt

With such wrong information
How can you be so proud
To keep running your mouth
And to do it so loud

Have you given thought
To how stupid you sound
Do you still talk this much
When there's no one around

Why don't you take a seat
Shut your mouth for a change
And give our ears a break
Before we all go insane?

Breaking Her Slowly

She hides her tears in public
Shies away from prying eyes
Makes a joke and laughs it off
While behind the mask, she dies

She tries to keep her head held high
To not let him see her break
But anyone who knows her knows
That the smile she wears is fake

Such an amazing person
With such a loving heart
But far too forgiving
And in need of a new start

So many years have gone by
And made her weak to him
He's worn her down and is content
To watch her sink while he swims

Every night it's insults thrown
And each word beats her down
Then come the apologies
But she can't make a sound

A walk throughout their dwelling
Tells a story of dismay
And if those walls could talk
Lord only knows what they would say

They'd probably tell tales
Of hardship and distrust
Of holes punched through the drywall
And all her things he chose to bust

But worst of all the casualties
Was her own self-worth
Her ability to love herself
Was what he went for first

Blinding her with hurtful words
Shattering her pride
Telling her she was no good
And she believed his lies

He broke her down so carefully
Whittling away
At all of her best qualities
Until slowly day by day

She started to agree with him
Found truth in every word
And she became a different person
Always seen but never heard

It took no time for him to break her
Make her think she couldn't leave
To suffocate her with his presence
Not give her any room to breath

Now years she feels she's wasted
Him still trying to remain
But finally she's realized
He isn't worth the pain

Not worth the isolation
From her family and her friends
So she pulls away from from him
Tries to begin again

It's hard in the beginning
To do it on her own
But in time she'll come to find
She's better off alone.

Why Bother?

Why do we bother trying
When giving up is easier
Why bother putting in the effort
When the people just get sleazier

No matter what they say
It always stays the same
Things will never change
It will always pour each time it rains

People never seem to grow
They refuse to lend a hand
They take without giving back
And when the well runs dry, don't understand

Selfish, arrogant, and blatantly rude
Not a care for those around them
Then when things go wrong they wonder
Why solitude surrounds them

They say that ignorance is bliss
That couldn't be more true
It's easy to be happy
When all you care about is you.

I Don't Know How

I know you look at me
And see someone you can fix
You think you see right through me
But you don’t know the half of it

And I’ve been here before
Down and out, in need of help
But my pain is not your burden
I can’t let you feel what I’ve felt

I’m not going to let you
Repair what you didn’t break
So even though I want to stay
It would be a big mistake

But you just keep on pushing
The more I pull away
You deserve an explanation
But I don’t know what to say

I don’t know how to tell you
The things you need to hear
And I can barely manage
To hold back my tears

We both know that you deserve more
Than what I can give you now
If I could I’d give you everything
But right now I don’t know how.

It Remains

What do you do
When things falls apart
When your world crumbles
And you're forced to restart

Do you hold on for dear life
Or let the past be the past
Do you try to forget
What you thought would last

How can you be expected
To stay tall and strong
When you're stuck in place
While they just keep moving on

They said it gets easier
It's not always this hard
So you just bite your tongue
And watch it from afar

But the pain never ceases
The heartache still remains
You watch their pain ease
While you still feel the same

Misguided and defeated
Left here on your own
Stuck in the dark
Trying to find your way home

But home never comes
Can't find your way back
Because home left with them
All they left was a crack

A crack deep in your heart
Leaving it ready to shatter
And the worst part is knowing
To them it doesn't matter

As you try to pick up the pieces
And save what remains
You cry and you question
If you'll get over the pain

But the pain never leaves
It forever stands strong
And you have to accept
That you'll never move on.

Way Up

What a world that we live in
There's nothing wonderful about it
Money makes the world turn
Can't get by without it

Turning people into monsters
Driven by their want
For everyone to know their names
To sit up at the top

Begging for your fifteen minutes
Hoping someone sees you
Telling anyone who'll listen
That there's nothing that you won't do

Everything's a stepping stone
The end will justify the means
Straight from the bottom to the top
Please excuse the inbetween

Everybody has a dream
And you can't catch a break
'Cause everybody wants something
And all they ever do is take

And you feel like fresh air is scarce
And maybe you might suffocate
Because trying to catch your breath
Is getting harder everyday

But even though they take from you
Until you have nothing left
And you can't help but notice
When you're at your worst they're at their best

You still feel like you're stuck there
And you can't walk away
The guilt would eat you from the inside out
Because you promised them you'd stay

And they don't notice that they're draining you
While filling their own cup
Because nothing else matters
When you're on your way up.

Not a Shit to Give

You can talk your shit
Go ahead and run your mouth
I've got more important things
To give a shit about

Your opinion is worth less to me
Than shit on the bottom of my shoe
And I could not care less about
What you think I should and shouldn't do

Last time I looked into it
You don't have a say
In the decisions that I make
How I live my life each day

It seems you struggle to remember
That the calls are mine to make
To think you have a say
Would be a big mistake

Your opinion means so little
When you won't say it to my face
And your advice is unsolicited
Save your breath 'cause it's a waste.

Undone

You think I'm just a little girl
That needs to be protected
So you're always on my heels
Even though you've been rejected

So quick to remind me of
All the mistakes I've made
Like I don't remember how it felt
When in that bed I laid

And when you aren't scolding me
For every choice I make
You're reminding me you've waited
So long for your chance to take

The shot that you've been hoping for
To get me in a ball and chain
And no matter how I protest
Your arguments the same

You've always been the "nice guy"
Content to finish last
The one who'd treat me right
Whose love would be unsurpassed

But all I hear is complaining
You're acting like a brat
Who's pissed that I don't feel the same
That all your efforts just fall flat

How can you be so confident
That you're just what I need
You think you know me oh so well
But you don't know a goddamn thing

Making passes at me
Every chance you get
Is not the way into my heart
Nor the way to get me wet

Maybe if you'd listened
If you'd really thought it through
I would have given you a chance back then
And wouldn't be with him instead of you

So consider this a lesson
We'll call it "Women 101"
Don't fall back into this pattern
Because mistakes can't be undone.

Icy

It’s easy to look down on me
From up on that high horse
But how can you be so awful
And not show any remorse

Does it make you feel better
About your pathetic little life
To use your words as tools
To cause other people strife

Some people want to watch
As the world burns
But you’re in line for that gas can
Just waiting for your turn

Is it that you’re jealous
That they’re everything you’re not
Or is it just because you’re bored
That you choose to stir the pot

Either way, if I were you
I’d keep an eye over my shoulder
‘Cause karma is an icy bitch
And she’ll just keep getting colder.

A Little Bit of Good

Everyone has good in them
At least that's what they say
But that gets harder to believe
With each passing day

It seems the good gets outweighed
By the lies, the sins, the greed
By people who are happy
To take more than what they need

Those who choose to squander
What they're fortunate to have
Who steal from those around them
Without ever looking back

They make up the majority
Of bad apples in the bunch
They take the heat off other ones
Whose edges are a little rough

The ones who thrive on white lies
Manipulation and deceit
The ones who get through life
By finding subtle ways to cheat

And so they go unnoticed
We choose to look away
Convince ourselves it's harmless
No one got hurt so it's okay

Just try to keep believing
People are inherently good
While we pretend we're not all liars
Excusing far more than we should

Will there ever come a time
When we'll get our shit together
Or will we continue down this path
Until the good is gone forever?

Bar None

Your life isn't all you'd hoped for
Nothing like the plans you made
All the dreams you used to have
You sat back and watched them fade

And now because you're pissed off
You blame everyone but you
Pointing fingers elsewhere
For everything you didn't do

Refusal to admit your faults
You push your opinions like they're facts
And spend your evenings rambling
About how if you could you would go back

Knowing what you know now
You'd choose a different path
Turn back the clock and start again
Not live in this aftermath

Of all your shitty choices
That you still refuse to own
You bitch non-stop about them
And wonder why you are alone

Maybe it's your attitude
Or all the lies you told
It might have been the bitterness
Or how easily you fold

To get your way, take what you want
And make sure you're saving face
But I think you'll find in all due time
That your pride cannot replace

The love you chose to throw away
When you decided you were right
When you chose to toss me aside
Because I wasn't worth the fight

And I hope you realize someday
All the damage that you've done
But for now enjoy your precious crown
For being "biggest bitch", bar none.

You'll Never Read This

I know you think you know him
But you don't know a thing
If you really knew him
You wouldn't wear that ring

You seem to think it's me
Who pines for his attention
But I cut him loose so long ago
Or did he forget to mention

That I kicked him to the curb
For more reasons that one
Or how he begged me not to leave him
When I told him I was done

I assume he hasn't told you
That he keeps me in his phone
And that I always get a message
Whenever he's alone

I know you think I start it
And it doesn't come as a surprise
That you blame everyone but him
For his wandering eyes

I'd hoped that it'd be clear to you
That I've moved on with my life
Now that I'm a grown ass women
A mother and a wife

Clear that I have no interest
In being anything to him
And I had so many reasons
For throwing the towel in

I've built a life I'm proud of
I have no reason to look back
You need to stop blaming me
For the loyalty he lacks

Believe me, I don't want him
You need to pay closer attention
Because I'm not the only person
To whom he tries to give affection

Maybe you should second guess
Who should hold the blame
Because we both know there are others
No matter what he claims

Your misplaced anger and distrust
Will only hurt you more
Maybe it's time to take his hand
And show him to the door

If you choose to stay with him
That's your choice to make
But you'll only have yourself to blame
When you notice your mistake

I truly hope that he gets better
And I wish you both the best
But do us all a favour
Give the shit you cause a rest

Don't worry about my life
Maybe pay attention to your own
Find out what he's doing
On your nights away from home

Because the unwanted advances
Are at no fault of mine
And I'm getting pretty tired
Of you both wasting my time

I think it's time I wrap this up
'Cause I've said all I need to say
But I suppose it doesn't matter
You'll never read this anyway.

Where Were You?

Where were you when I needed you
When I was on my own
When I was broken down and lost
So far away from home

When everything was new again
And I was starting from square one
I had nothing, I had no one
And that's when you chose to run

You stuck around for good times
But dipped when shit hit the fan
You disappeared for so long
I didn't think I'd hear from you again

Not a word to me or mine
But content to tell my story
When I called you on your bullshit
All you had to say was sorry

And time and time again
I let you back into to my life
Made the same mistake
Gave you back the knife

Guess I misjudged you greatly
Thought I knew you so well
But I've seen your true colours
And you can go to hell.

You Know It

I work my ass off
And you know it
Try my damnedest
But still blow it

I do my best
I tow the line
But when I excel
You still find

An excuse to pass me over
A reason to deny me
To say it's not enough
A way to nullify me

Judge me by my cover
Not by the contents of each page
Decide you know me best
Based on my looks, my friends, my age

Assume because you're older
That you must be wiser, too
But that kind of arrogance
Ain't a good look for you

Just keep the judgement coming
Enjoy your high horse while it lasts
'Cause when karma makes her rounds
She'll be coming for your ass.

Looking Back

It's funny how we look back
And see how much we've changed
We wonder where the time went
And see who's left us and who stayed

Some notes between old friends
And a handful of old pictures
Bring back memories of a time
When things were so much simpler

Now best friends are strangers
And strangers are best friends
Making promises that they won't keep
Like they'll be there 'til the end

They say that life's not measured
By the amount of breaths we take
Rather it's measured by the moments
That take our breath away

Though merely sixty seconds
Is all a minute holds
It seems some moments last forever
In our memories they're bold

Looking back I wonder
Where that part of my life went
The friends, the clothes, the memories
The things I won't forget

But it doesn't matter how we try
To hold onto what we had
Everyone moves on
And has to leave it in the past

We used to sit outside for hours
We'd laugh and mess around
The days went on forever
Lasting long past sundown

Then along came college
Houses, jobs, and kids
We all went our separate ways
And forgot all that we did

Friends that were inseparable
Now barely say hello
And friends that said forever
Have since let that promise go

It seems like all good times
Last just a little while
But I hope now and then you think of me
And it leaves you with a smile

Because every so often
For many years to come
I'll think of you and smile
And remember all we've done.

Belief in Love

I'm staring at a blank page
The right words evade my mind
All that I can think about
Is how I never thought I'd find

The person who would love me
Regardless of my past
The person who would care enough
To try and make it last

Then you came along
And you helped me up
Too good to be true
It had to be dumb luck

But you stuck around
You gave me your heart
And I know without you
I would fall apart

In all the good I see
Every melody I hear
Each happy thought I have
You are always there

You're my reason to wake up each day
And never throw the fight
And I see your eyes
Within the stars at night

Your smile became the light
That guides me through the dark
And your love became the glue
That mends my broken heart

In your arms I am invincible
I know I'm safe and lived
And I know you'll always be there
When push comes to shove

When you came into my life
You gave me a new start
And in return for yours
I gave you my heart
When I look into your eyes
I can see forever
And the minute that you kiss me
Everything feels better

You fix all that goes wrong
You save me from myself
You hold me while I cry
No matter what about

Now I know it's real
I can see it in your eyes
I hear it in your voice
Feel it when you're by my side

You've changed my whole life
Mere words will never be enough
To thank you for restoring
My belief in love.

Good On My Own

I am who I am
So fuck what you say
I'll be who I want
And do shit my own way

If you don't like it
I guess that's too bad
'Cause trying to change me
Will drive you mad

My life is my own
So butt the fuck out
Mind your own business
Keep your thoughts to yourself

Do me a favour
Keep my name out of your mouth
And when you fuck up
Don't come asking for help

I don't need your nagging
Or the shit that you start
I don't need you here
Trying to tear me apart

It’s time you piss off
And leave me alone
I don’t need your help
I’m good on my own.

Not Worth Saving

Had more than enough
It's become too much
Never thought I'd have to say goodbye

You made the choice
I lost my voice
After all the tears I've cried

I've given up
You took too much
Now I can barely breathe

Wasn't ready for this
For our last kiss
Why did you have to leave

Pain in my chest
Gives me no rest
On the edge I'm swaying

No longer alive
Dead inside
My life is not worth saving.

Seem Alive

A constant battle in my mind
Each day I face myself
Looking from the outside in
You would never know

Tears held back in public
No matter how it burns
My battle is internal
You'll never see my wounds

Though I wear a painted smile
My eyes give me away
But most will never notice
And those who do will never say

My lifeline's wearing thin
Each word stings like a smack
I teeter at the edge
Wind blowing hard against my back

Yet each day I still wake up
And keep pushing to survive
Though I feel dead inside
I fight to seem alive.

Let It Die

You had no reason
Had no right
To cheat me of
A normal life

You give so little
But take so much
Do what you want
Break my trust

Lean on me
When you need help
'Cause you know you've got
No one else

You wonder why
You're on your own
And why I don't
Pick up the phone

You played your games
And had your fun
Only looked out
For number one

Your words were used as weapons
The stories twisted for your gain
I was warned about you
Warned you'd never change

Warned that your top priority
Would always be yourself
You'd take what you want from me
And not care how I felt

Now you're here expecting me
To clean the mess you made
Why should it fall on me to fix
What you chose to break

Because your pride is always most important
And your ego isn't small
Lying through your teeth
You think you've fooled us all

But I see through your bullshit
And won't let you win this one
You won't make me the bad guy
This time I'm fucking done

Won't be stuck in the middle
Where each tear shed burns my eyes
Why should I revive this
When you're the one who let it die?

www.ingramcontent.com/pod-product-compliance
Lightning Source LLC
Chambersburg PA
CBHW051740130826
49812CB00033B/940
* 9 7 8 9 3 5 7 2 1 3 2 9 5 *